DARING WOMEN OF D-DAY

Bold Spies of WORLD WAR II

by Jen Breach   illustrated by Alessia Trunfio

CAPSTONE PRESS
a capstone imprint

Published by Capstone Press, an imprint of Capstone
1710 Roe Crest Drive, North Mankato, Minnesota 56003
capstonepub.com

Library of Congress Cataloging-in-Publication Data
Names: Breach, Jen, author. | Trunfio, Alessia, 1990– illustrator.
Title: Daring women of D-day : bold spies of World War II / by Jen Breach ; illustrated by Alessia Trunfio. Other titles: Bold spies of World War II
Description: North Mankato, Minnesota : Capstone Press, an imprint of Capstone, [2024] | Series: Women warriors of World War II | Includes bibliographical references. | Audience: Ages 8–11 | Audience: Grades 4–6 | Summary: "An action-packed graphic novel about agents who helped the Allies prepare for D-Day and push the Germans out of France during World War II. In 1942, World War II was growing more and more intense. Germany and its allies had occupied a great deal of Europe—including part of France. With the enemy just a few miles from England, Prime Minister Winston Churchill was determined to help free France. To make his plan work, he needed people who could secretly help prepare the French for a big fight. He found 39 daring women who were up to the task—including Andrée Borrel and Lise de Baissac. These women would help support the French Resistance and sabotage German operations in preparation for the 1944 D-Day invasion. In this full-color graphic novel, discover more about these bold women who helped free France from German occupation during World War II"—Provided by publisher.
Identifiers: LCCN 2023002019 (print) | LCCN 2023002020 (ebook) |
ISBN 9781669013624 (hardcover) | ISBN 9781669013570 (paperback) |
ISBN 9781669013587 (ebook pdf) | ISBN 9781669013600 (kindle edition) |
ISBN 9781669013617 (epub)
Subjects: LCSH: World War, 1939–1945—Secret service—Great Britain—Comic books, strips, etc.—Juvenile literature. | Women spies—Great Britain—History—20th century—Comic books, strips, etc.—Juvenile literature. | Spies—Great Britain—History—20th century—Comic books, strips, etc.—Juvenile literature. | Espionage, British—France—History—20th century—Comic books, strips, etc.—Juvenile literature. | Borrel, Andrée, 1919–1944—Comic books, strips, etc.—Juvenile literature. | Baissac, Lise de, 1905–2004—Comic books, strips, etc.—Juvenile literature. | World War, 1939–1945—Underground movements—France—Comic books, strips, etc.—Juvenile literature.
Classification: LCC D810.S7 B663 2024 (print) | LCC D810.S7 (ebook) |
DDC 940.54/8641082—dc23/eng/20230118
LC record available at https://lccn.loc.gov/2023002019
LC ebook record available at https://lccn.loc.gov/2023002020

Editorial Credits
Editor: Ericka Smith; Designer: Sarah Bennett; Production Specialist: Katy LaVigne

Design Elements: Shutterstock/Here

All internet sites appearing in back matter were available and accurate when this book was sent to press.

Direct quotations appear in bold italicized text on the following pages:
Pages 21, 29: from *D-Day Girls: The Spies Who Armed the Resistance, Sabotaged the Nazis, and Helped Win World War II*, by Sarah Rose. New York: Crown, 2019.

TABLE OF CONTENTS

A PROBLEM IN FRANCE

London, 1942

British Prime Minister Winston Churchill had a problem—three years after World War II had begun, German troops had occupied many of the surrounding countries in Europe.

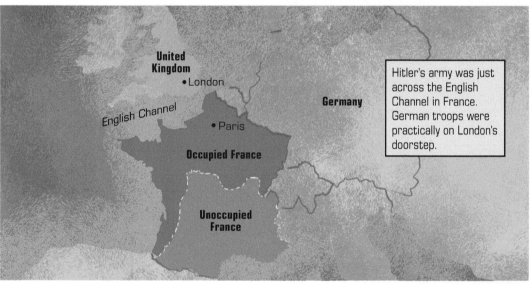

United Kingdom
• London

English Channel

• Paris

Germany

Occupied France

Unoccupied France

Hitler's army was just across the English Channel in France. German troops were practically on London's doorstep.

Churchill and his allies planned to free France. It would be a massive operation and take a full year to prepare. The date hadn't been picked yet, but it was already called D-Day.

Allied soldiers would land on France's beaches. French rebels who had been trained by British spies would attack the German army from inland.
But with so many men serving in the military, who could serve as spies?

We simply can't spare any men.

What if we sent women instead?

Women?! Are you mad?

Women are already contributing to the war effort. They work, they volunteer, they make sacrifices. And women would be less suspicious.

The Special Operations Executive had already begun searching for British women who could speak perfect French.

If we find women who can speak French, they'll blend right in and help prepare the French for a fight.

Hmm. You might be onto something.

5

THE WORLD'S FIRST FEMALE PARATROOPERS

Andrée Borrel and Lise de Baissac were among 39 women who answered the call. They were trained, but not as soldiers. Women could not enlist at that time.

They were taught how to clean and shoot guns, how to set C-4 explosives, and how to withstand interrogation.

This is much better than working in an office!

Parisian-born Andrée started fighting for France when the German army began its occupation of Paris in 1940. Tough and self-reliant, Andrée ran a safe house that helped smuggle British soldiers back to London. In 1942, she was betrayed, but was able to escape.

But she loved France. She was ready to go back.

Lise grew up wealthy in Mauritius, a French-speaking British colony. Smart, brave, and athletic, she aced her training.

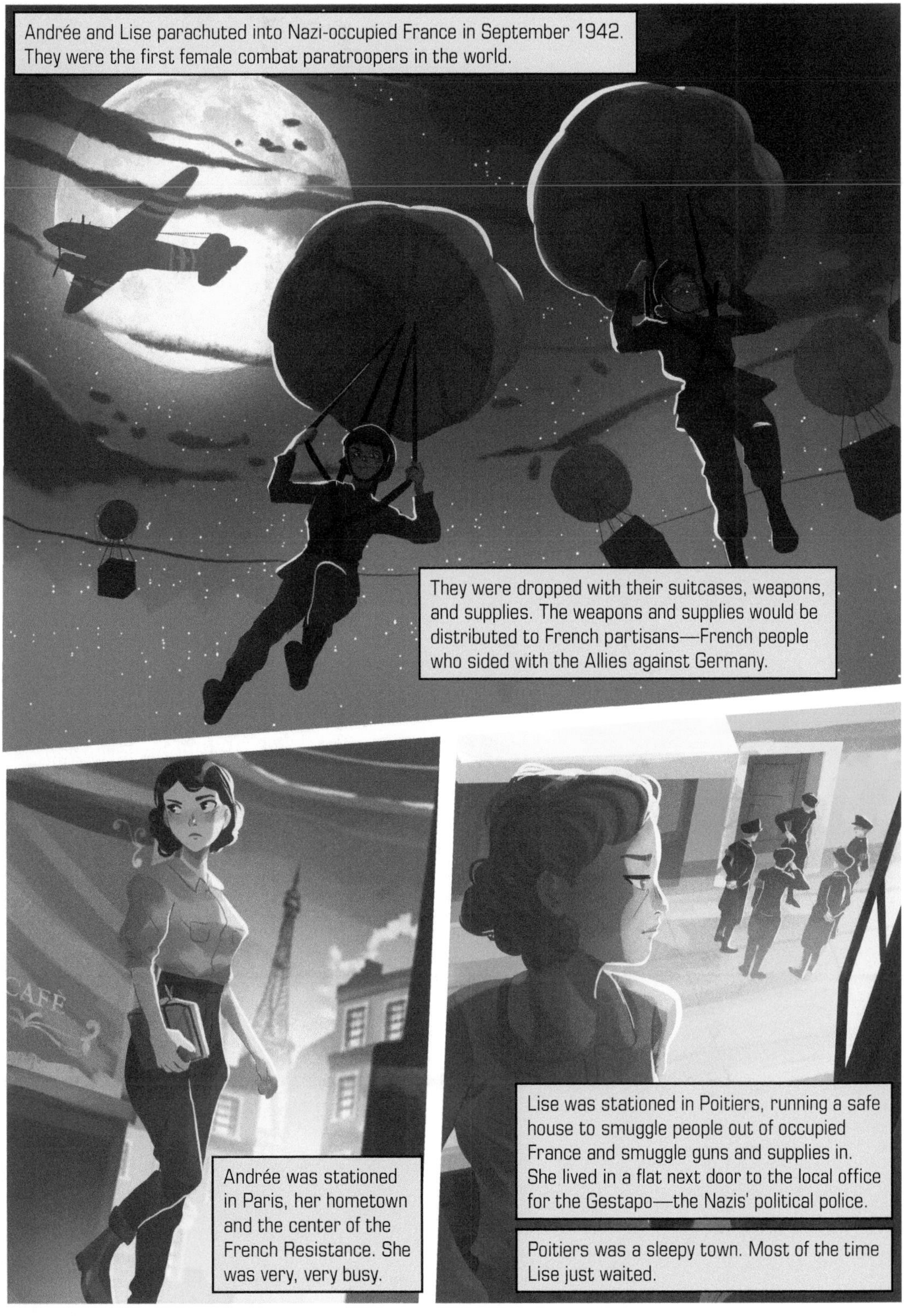
Andrée and Lise parachuted into Nazi-occupied France in September 1942. They were the first female combat paratroopers in the world.
They were dropped with their suitcases, weapons, and supplies. The weapons and supplies would be distributed to French partisans—French people who sided with the Allies against Germany.
CAFÉ
Andrée was stationed in Paris, her hometown and the center of the French Resistance. She was very, very busy.
Lise was stationed in Poitiers, running a safe house to smuggle people out of occupied France and smuggle guns and supplies in. She lived in a flat next door to the local office for the Gestapo—the Nazis' political police.
Poitiers was a sleepy town. Most of the time Lise just waited.

ANDRÉE THE COURIER

In Paris, Andrée carried messages between her French partisan network and British agents.

Right under the nose of the German army.

Andrée was part of a small team that included Francis, the head of covert operations in the Paris area, and a radio operator named Gilbert.

What have you got for me, Francis?

Lots, I'm afraid. Messages for Gilbert.

Another glorious day fighting the Nazis!

France had been occupied for two years when Andrée returned. There were small pockets of French partisans and daily acts of rebellion in Paris.

Francis and Andrée's mission was to coordinate and arm these rebels ahead of D-Day.

PAS DE NAZIS EN FRANCE

The French rebellion relied on radio transmissions to and from London. Messages included codes for an agent and an action or operation. They would say things like "The dog sneezed on the curtains." Even if the Germans listened in, they didn't know what it meant.

Radio operators like Gilbert had to code and decode messages on the fly.

Good morning, Gilbert!

Is it ever!

Gilbert operated radios stashed around Paris. They had to be moved all the time so that the Gestapo could not track him.

So every day Andrée walked and cycled miles around Paris. She carried codes, messages, radio parts and more, right past German soldiers and their French collaborators.

The farms and villages surrounding Paris were also a part of Andrée's network.

French partisans, who wouldn't collaborate with the Germans, suffered terribly under occupation, especially poor people in the countryside.

Hitler sent most of the food grown on French farms to German troops fighting in Russia. The farmers were hungry—and angry.

Andrée knew how important these everyday people were to the rebellion. Food and guns helped, and so did a listening ear for their troubles.

Some were the mothers of young men who had been enslaved and forced to work in German factories.

Our son was sent away! It wasn't enough he had to work for Hitler in a French factory. They packed him off to work in a German one!

I am so sorry!

Others were French Jews who had been stripped of property and the right to work. Many were sent to German concentration camps.

It's not much, but I hope this helps.

Andrée's work was very dangerous. British agents captured in France were not treated as prisoners of war.

When found, British agents in France were tortured for information and killed.

Everything seems in order.

Of course.

ANDRÉE THE SABOTEUR

Andrée's work followed the phases of the moon. Full moons were for connecting with her network and for supply drops.

Any second now.

Do you hear that?

Let's go!

Each drop was met by a reception committee. Many female British agents like Andrée and Lise managed reception committees of local partisans.

The French Resistance relied on the drops. They included essentials like . . .

. . . food . . .

. . . guns and plastic explosives . . .

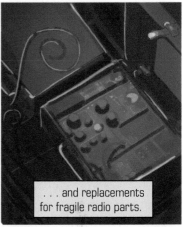

. . . and replacements for fragile radio parts.

Andrée's team could quickly break down and repack the supplies, bury the parachutes, and disappear into the night. They left no trace.

We'll put these to use!

Andrée's team also carried out "bangs." These were sabotage missions that often involved blowing things up.

They might also cut German communication lines or disable trains.

Tra la la la. Nothing to see here.

Bangs were an important part of the preparation for D-Day. They boosted the morale of the French partisans.

There they are, Jean!

And they were annoying and inconvenient for the German army.

Tra la la la!

One bang was blowing up electricity transformers that powered the east-west railroad, which carried German troops and supplies from Berlin to the French coast.

It was important that bangs never harmed French people. They were very carefully planned and executed.

Andrée and Jean laid out the plastic explosives. Andrée set the detonators . . .

Easy does it.

. . . and they hurried away.

At the same time, other teams were doing the same thing. It would be quite a mess for the Germans.

KABOOM!

What a lovely day for a bang.

PING! SNAP!

None of Andrée's network were caught that day.

It took weeks for the German army to get the electricity back on.

THE GESTAPO GETS TWITCHY

After nearly a year of planning, the message from London in Spring 1943 was "Be ready."

Andrée and her network were busy with more drops than ever.

Orders from London were for more and more bangs too.

Andrée's network leapt into action. It was exhausting work.

But morale in the Resistance was high.

During the Nazis' occupation of France, the Gestapo would constantly change ID requirements for French citizens.

Every time they did, Andrée and Gilbert had to make hundreds of fake IDs.

It was costly and time-consuming to create new fake IDs. But without them, Andrée's network could not move around freely and safely.

In June 1943, the Gestapo changed the ID requirements in France yet again.

The Germans like to annoy us as much as we annoy them.

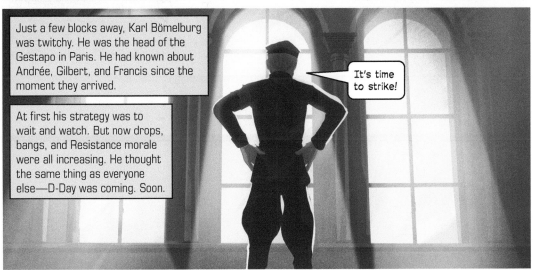

Just a few blocks away, Karl Bömelburg was twitchy. He was the head of the Gestapo in Paris. He had known about Andrée, Gilbert, and Francis since the moment they arrived.

At first his strategy was to wait and watch. But now drops, bangs, and Resistance morale were all increasing. He thought the same thing as everyone else—D-Day was coming. Soon.

It's time to strike!

By June 23, 1943, Andrée and Gilbert had run out of time and luck.

You're under arrest!

Andrée shoved her list of agents into her mouth.

She tried to jump out the window.

Nein!

The Gestapo seized Andrée's fake ID materials. They suddenly knew the identities of hundreds of partisans in Andrée's network.

Andrée was tortured for days for more information. But she never talked.

Because of her flawless French, the Gestapo thought Andrée was a Parisian partisan—not a British spy. Instead of being murdered, she was sent to Fresnes Prison in Paris.

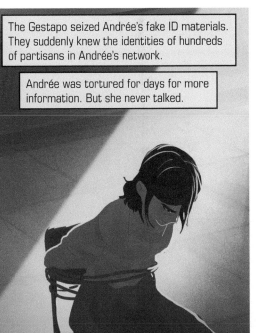

Over the next weeks, hundreds of British agents and French partisans were arrested in France.

About a third of the Resistance fighters and weapons were seized. The British agents who weren't arrested fled to London. Bömelburg had crippled the French Resistance.

D-Day could not go ahead. And it would take almost a year for the French Resistance to rebuild.

LISE GOES TO NORMANDY

By the summer of 1944, Allied forces were finally ready for D-Day. All eyes were on the sleepy seaside towns of Normandy.

The D-Day landing in Normandy was a huge undertaking. On June 6, 1944, about 156,000 Allied troops crossed the English Channel. By June 11, more than 326,000 Alied troops would move inland through Normandy to liberate France and head for Berlin.

Churchill had promised that D-Day would be the end of the war. But it took the Allied forces weeks just to fight their way off the beaches.

Lise was in Normandy then, working as second-in-command to her brother Claude, the head of the French Resistance there. They made a good team, and Lise was happy to be useful.

That summer, Lise was caught in a firefight with a German patrol.

If you're frightened, you can't do anything.

She fought bravely and survived the conflict.

While Allied troops fought on the beach all summer, Lise managed her network behind enemy lines.

HUFF.
HUFF. HUFF.

They kept morale up among the French partisans. They carried out "bangs" almost every day, and they kept London informed of German troop movements.

Lise bicycled long distances each day. She was regularly stopped by German soldiers.

Like Andrée, she carried messages and delivered radio parts. If she was caught, she would be killed.

But she was never caught.

You may pass.

Merci.

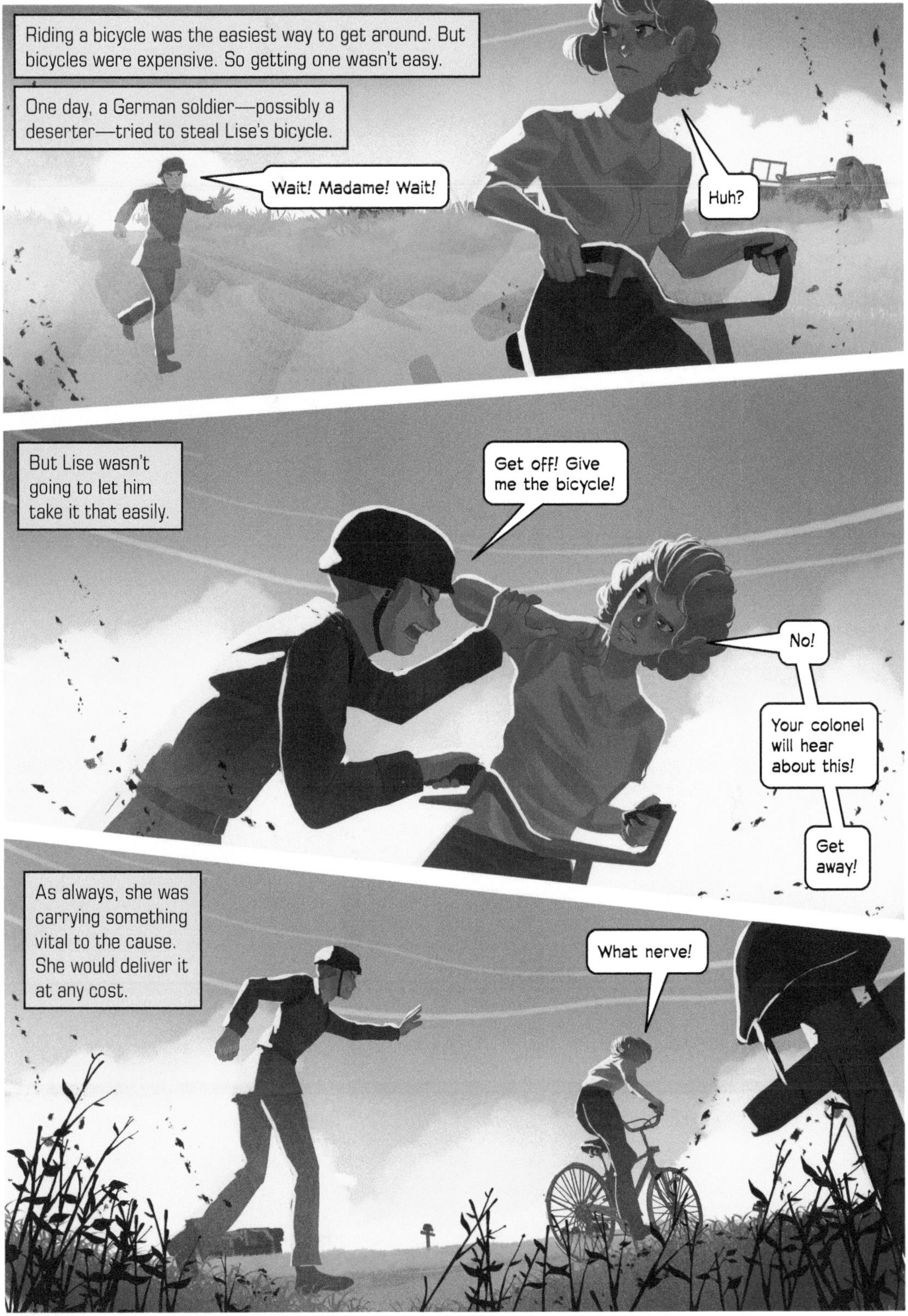
Riding a bicycle was the easiest way to get around. But bicycles were expensive. So getting one wasn't easy.
One day, a German soldier—possibly a deserter—tried to steal Lise's bicycle.
Wait! Madame! Wait!
Huh?
But Lise wasn't going to let him take it that easily.
Get off! Give me the bicycle!
No!
Your colonel will hear about this!
Get away!
As always, she was carrying something vital to the cause. She would deliver it at any cost.
What nerve!

The base of Lise's network was in Saint-Mars-du-Désert—more than 150 miles (241 kilometers) from the fighting on the beaches.

Home, sweet home.

In August 1944, the Allied armies pushed the German army back through the village of Saint-Mars-du-Désert.

As the Germans retreated, they commandeered places to stay.

German soldiers commandeered the schoolhouse where Lise and Claude ran their network.

They never knew what it had been used for.

The soldiers commandeered Lise's apartment too. She was angry, but she couldn't risk being caught.

You have one minute to gather your things.

We are honorable and will not steal your things.

CLICK

You better not.

Here.

HUMPH!

If the captain had looked in the cupboard, he would have found English tea.

It could have gotten Lise killed.

Phew!

THE MISSION ENDS

After the Germans left the village, the Allied forces followed close on their heels.

After more than two months of fighting, the Germans were finally driven out of Normandy.

Lise had seen so much, *done* so much. But now her mission was over.

When the Allied forces liberated Paris in August 1944, Andrée was already gone. One month after D-Day, Andrée had been sent to Natzweiler-Struthof, the only concentration camp on French soil.

On July 6, 1944, Andrée was murdered by poisonous injection at Natzweiler-Struthof. She was 24 years old.

She had spent four years fighting, but never got to see her beloved Paris liberated.

NOT JUST CIVILIANS

Fourteen of the 39 British women who served as organizers and saboteurs in France died there. Most were tortured.

Some female agents, like Lise, were brought back to England quickly. Others were harder to find.

While enlisted men could be accounted for, female spies were civilians. They had pretended to be French so well that they could not prove they were British.

Churchill did not want to give away his strategy, so he wouldn't release their names to help locate them.

One female agent wasn't brought home to England until 11 months after Paris's liberation.

After the war, enlisted men received military honors—including British agents stationed in France.

Women had not been able to enlist in the British military, so Lise and other female agents were not eligible for military honors or pensions.

Lise's civilian award was for "gallantry not in the face of the enemy."

Not all women who served would accept the award.

Pearl Witherington Cornioley was a British agent in occupied France. She had led a rebel force of 1,500 men and oversaw the surrender of about 18,000 Germans after D-Day. She refused her civilian honors.

There was nothing remotely civil about what I did.

And British agents weren't the only women fighting in France.

All in all, there were about 200,000 Allied-backed partisans who fought to liberate France after D-Day. Many of them were women.

GLOSSARY

agent (AY-jent)—a spy

Allies (AL-eyes)—a group of countries that fought together in World War II, including the United States, England, France, and the Soviet Union

collaborator (kuh-LAB-uh-ray-tur)—a person who secretly helps an enemy

commandeer (kom-un-DEER)—to take control of for use by the military

covert (koh-VURT)—secret

Gestapo (guh-STAH-poh)—the secret political police of Nazi Germany

morale (muh-RAL)—a person or group's feelings or state of mind

network (NET-wurk)—a system of people or things that cross or connect

occupy (OK-yuh-pahy)—to take possession or control by military invasion

partisan (PAHR-tuh-zuhn)—someone who helps fight against an occupying military

rebel (REB-uhl)—someone who fights against a government or the people in charge of something

sabotage (SAB-uh-tahzh)—to damage, destroy, or disrupt on purpose

saboteur (sab-uh-TUR)—someone who damages, destroys, or disrupts on purpose

smuggle (SMUHG-uhl)—to bring something or someone into or out of a country secretly and often illegally

READ MORE

Berglund, Bruce. *Night Witches at War: The Soviet Women Pilots of World War II*. North Mankato, MN: Capstone, 2020.

Gunderson, Jessica. *Nancy Wake: Fearless Spy of World War II*. North Mankato, MN: Capstone, 2022.

Ruelle, Karen Gray. *Surprising Spies: Unexpected Heroes of World War II*. New York: Holiday House, 2020.

INTERNET SITES

DK Find Out!: French Resistance
dkfindout.com/uk/history/world-war-ii/french-resistance

The National WWII Museum: D-Day Fact Sheet
nationalww2museum.org/media/press-releases/d-day-fact-sheet-0

Time: The Extraordinary Bravery That Made This Woman One of World War II's Most Remarkable Spies
time.com/5502645/decorated-wwii-spy-odette

ABOUT THE AUTHOR

Jen Breach (they/them) grew up queer and nonbinary in rural Australia with three big brothers, two parents, and one pet duck. Jen has worked as a bagel baker, a codebreaker, a ticket taker, and a troublemaker. They now work as a writer—the best job ever—in Philadelphia, Pennsylvania.

ABOUT THE ILLUSTRATOR

Alessia Trunfio is a children's book illustrator. After graduating in Animation from the International School of Comics in 2013 in Rome, she worked as a background artist for some of the most important animation studios. After a few years she decided to start a career as an illustrator. She currently works with the New York illustrator agency Astound and has published for many international publishers.